Not My Family

Not My Family:

Sharing the Truth about Alcoholism

by Maxine B. Rosenberg

BRADBURY PRESS   NEW YORK

Bradbury Press
An Affiliate of Macmillan, Inc.
866 Third Avenue, New York, NY 10022
Collier Macmillan Canada, Inc.
First Edition
Printed in the United States of America
10 9 8 7 6 5 4 3 2 1

The text of this book is set in 12 point Baskerville.
Book design by Julie Quan

LIBRARY OF CONGRESS CATALOGING-IN-PUBLICATION DATA
Rosenberg, Maxine B.
Not my family.
Bibliography: p.
Includes index.
1. Children of alcoholics—United States—Attitudes.
2. Adult children of alcoholics—United States—
Attitudes.   3. Alcoholics—United States—Family
relationships.   I. Title.
HV5132.R68 1988   362.2'92   88-10468
ISBN 0-02-777911-4

ACKNOWLEDGMENTS

My grateful thanks to the following people and organizations: Project Rainbow, Pomona, New York — John Slotwinski and Jean Pickerelli, for their time and encouragement in helping me organize my ideas for this book; Week-end Center, Mt. Kisco, New York, for trusting me with their children and lending me their facilities; Unicorn Program, Peekskill, New York; Rabbi Daniel Isaacs and Reverend Jack Miller, for leading me to the right sources; Sharon Steinhoff, my editor, for being there all the way and then some more; my children—Mark, David, Seth, and Karin—for their interest and patience; and most of all to my husband, Paul, for his encouragement, understanding, and utmost support.

To Sylvia Rosenblum — who understands

CONTENTS

Not My Family

INTRODUCTION

When most people hear the word "alcoholic," they imagine a derelict lying in the street. Actually, there are very few Skid Row alcoholics compared to the total number of people addicted to alcohol in our society. Indeed, alcoholism is a disease that can affect any person, of any ethnic group, living anywhere in the world.

According to the National Association for Children of Alcoholics, an estimated twenty-eight million children have at least one alcoholic parent. Looked at another way, one out of three families reports living with an alcohol abuser. Not surprisingly, then, the latest Gallup poll indicates that problem drinking has reached its highest level in thirty-seven years.

Alcoholism, like cancer, has a variety of possible causes, ranging from family tendency to environmental factors. Its symptoms vary from individual to individual, but all alcoholics share an inability to control their drinking. The difference between abuse and alcoholism is not in the quantity consumed but in the person's addiction to it. Besides creating anguish for the addicted, alcoholism causes enormous pain for all those closely involved.

Until ten years ago, people paid little attention to the effects of a parent's alcoholism on a child. They concentrated more on curing the drinker's problem. Now it's clear that the problems caused by a parent's drinking do not evaporate with sobriety. Even adult children of alcoholics admit to continuing difficulties, such as poor self-image and feelings of distrust and guilt. Furthermore, over one hundred published studies support the theory that alcoholism tends to run in families, and that children of alcoholics are at much greater risk than the average population of becoming alcoholic or marrying someone who drinks.

One of my hopes in writing this book is that it will help children of alcoholics, young and old, to realize they are not alone. Too many of these children have kept their family situation a secret, out of both shame and a desire to remain loyal to their parents. By denying their parents' alcoholism or distancing themselves from it, these children thought they could escape the pain and trauma of their home life. But years later they woke up, only to find that their fears and sadness had followed them.

When I started to work on this book, I realized how

little first-hand experience I had with children living in an alcoholic home. I am not a child of an alcoholic, nor are any of my relatives or close friends, except for one friend who chooses to share little about that part of her life.

Before I began interviewing, I did research in the library, where I pored through books, magazines, and journals for background information. Then I located the nearest Adult Children of Alcoholics (ACOA) group and attended its meetings. There I heard ACOA members describe the impact their parents' alcoholism had on them. At the same time I attended conferences on alcoholism and met with private therapists and professionals at treatment centers, who further explained the trauma a parent's drinking causes a child.

As I spoke to people about my book, more and more enthusiasm for it mounted. "I wish I had had something like that to help me when I was a kid," one man said. "Instead, I waited until I was thirty-five to discover there were others like me." Still other adult children of alcoholics telephoned and asked if I could interview them, not necessarily wanting to appear in the book, just aching to be heard.

I have used four stories told to me by members of the ACOA group I observed. All of these adult children have regularly attended meetings a few times a week for a period of one to four years. At some time in their adult life, each also sought private counseling. The two other adult children in this book are a professional acquaintance and someone who was referred to me.

All the young children were recommended to me by counselors working at treatment centers or in schools. Before the counselors offered a child's name, they asked the parents to discuss the project at home and to consider how the family would feel about having their story in print. Only one family, of those queried, declined.

Although I interviewed many more people than the fourteen who appear in this book, I could not, for obvious reasons, include all the stories. Still, each person's ideas and experiences enriched this project.

To oblige their wish for privacy, I met all the adult interviewees in their own homes. By contrast, three of the children chose to meet at their after-school treatment center. I told the children their interviews would take no longer than forty-five minutes, and the adults were asked to set aside an hour and a half. In the end, most interviews lasted more than twice the intended time. "Stay longer," an eleven-year-old boy urged. "Are you sure there's nothing else you want to ask me?" The adults, too, were anxious to talk. "Getting out my feelings makes me feel much better. You helped me remember incidents I thought I had forgotten," one man said.

While most of the adults had little difficulty describing their lives and the effect their parents' alcoholism had on them, many of the children—the younger ones, in particular—needed more time and encouragement to open up and trust me. To relax, they drew pictures as they talked, and then we played with cards, checkers, or puppets.

As the adults and children talked, many agreed that today, more than ever before, alcoholics are receiving encouragement to control their disease. In addition, with formerly addicted celebrities sharing their stories, more alcoholics are realizing they are not alone. Furthermore, children in alcoholic families are now more likely to accept that they need not be ashamed of their family situation or feel responsible for causing it.

But along with these positive strides in our society come mixed messages. On the one hand, television campaigns and newspaper advertising urge alcoholics and their families to seek treatment. Meanwhile, numerous ads continue to portray drinking as a way to relax and have fun. Even more confusing, many people view alcohol use—and abuse—as a coming-of-age experience, which makes it acceptable.

Luckily, the children in this book have been discussing the influences on their attitudes toward drinking with their counselors and peers. In so doing, they have gained a maturity and wisdom beyond their years.

Everyone to whom I spoke—both children and adults—considered themselves fortunate for having found someone trustworthy to confide in. With industriousness, determination, and inner strength, they have finally begun to break the chain that might have damaged their families for generations. When asked what advice they would give others in their same situation, all suggested finding a caring person to talk to.

Although many of the adults I interviewed learned only recently where their sadness and fears originated, each emphasized that it's never too late to change. As one sixty-two-year-old child of an alcoholic said, "I've got many more years to have fun. No sense in keeping all these troubles to myself."

Most of the younger children began discovering the source of their problems from a school or treatment center counselor. But a caring teacher, a pastor, a friend's parent, a relative—all are good people for children of alcoholics to turn to. And many teenagers recommend organizations like Alateen and ACOA.

While it's not easy to erase the sadness that has colored the lives of so many children of alcoholics, it's still possible to learn to laugh, to love, to forgive. And, with time, impossible dreams start to come true.

"I love the feeling of being on top of the world"

JORI, age 11

"Since Dad went into recovery three years ago, my whole life seems better. I actually have fun most of the time, and that's not how it used to be. Now, when I introduce Dad to my friends, I'm happy to show him off." Jori beams.

Jori's father started drinking when he was a teenager, even though his own father had died of alcoholism years before. He continued drinking despite a serious car accident while drunk. When Jori was born, alcoholism was already part of her family.

"Until three years ago, I can't remember a time Dad didn't drink," Jori says. "Now and then he stopped, and I'd get hopeful, but a few days later he returned to the bottle. When Dad drank, he used to blame me for anything that went wrong. And he had a terrible temper. I hated the yelling.

"Whenever I could, I got out of the house. Sometimes I ran with my little sister, Morgan, to our neighbor's apartment and stayed there until my parents stopped arguing. Or I went by myself to the playground. I'd say, 'I'm going out, Mom,' and then I would leave without waiting for permission."

More than once Jori appealed to her father to stop drinking. "'It's bad for you,' I'd say, but he'd answer, 'Don't tell me what to do.' I would have hidden his bottles, but I was too scared," she admits.

Despite her father's drinking, Jori excelled in school and made high honors each year. When she started playing the violin in first grade, she discovered it helped her relax. "In the beginning, I felt discouraged because I made so many mistakes. But then I got better at it and found that playing certain kinds of music made me feel good. Now, if I want to get in a happy mood, I pick up the violin and fiddle away."

Soon after Jori's eighth birthday, her parents separated for nine months. Her father moved to a tiny apartment and the two girls stayed with their mother. Jori was miserable. "No matter what had gone on at home, I didn't want Dad to leave the family because I was afraid I'd never see him again. With all his problems, I still cared about him and wanted him to live with us. I remember feeling so awful and alone at that time. There was no one I could talk to, or at least that was what I thought."

In school, Jori's grades suddenly plummeted. "I

became real quiet, after being a noisy kid my whole life. My teacher sent me to the school counselor, who played games with me about feelings. It didn't take long before I blurted out what was on my mind. Boy, did I feel better," Jori recalls.

Meanwhile Jori's mother started speaking to someone at an alcoholic treatment center, and Jori's father decided to give up drinking.

After three years of talking about the effects of alcoholism on her family, Jori now realizes she did not cause her father's disease, nor could she have done anything to control it.

"I know now that Dad stopped drinking when *he* wanted to. Nobody forced him; he made the decision. I think the main reason he quit was that he wanted to be back with the family, especially Mom. He was unhappy when he lived alone. It took me awhile to believe I had no part in doing those bad things Dad did to himself. What a relief to learn that!"

Since Jori's father has been in recovery, Jori says she feels freer choosing her special interests. "Before, when Dad drank I did things to get rid of anger or to relax. Now I jog or ice-skate just because I love it, and I play the violin because it makes me happy," she explains.

Another big change in her life is the number of people invited to her house. Without the tension and the drinking, Jori no longer feels embarrassed to have her friends over. And the holidays, especially, are often shared with relatives or close friends. "My grandpar-

ents came for Passover," Jori says proudly, "and everything was peaceful. I probably was the most nervous
when I realized the mustard salad dressing had wine in
it. Since Dad's been in recovery, he's very cautious
about what he eats. Before we buy any special food, he
reads the ingredients to make sure there's no liquor in
it. At my aunt's wedding, Dad tasted some alcohol in
the chocolate cake and wouldn't eat it. I didn't notice a
thing and ate the whole piece." She laughs.

Today, much of Jori's family life still centers around
alcoholism. Her father goes to Alcoholics Anonymous
(AA) meetings four days a week, and her mother
attends Al-Anon, an organization for the family and
friends of alcoholics, on Monday and Friday evenings.
Jori and her sister go to the alcoholic treatment center
once a week. "I wish my family had more time to spend
with each other, but right now I know what we're doing
is more important," Jori says.

Despite the number of changes in her life, Jori con-
tinues to find it difficult to share her feelings with most
people. "At the treatment center, I say whatever I want
about anything, especially to my friend Kendel. But I'd
like my mother to be a mind reader and say, 'I know
what's troubling you, sweetheart. It's okay. It's not your
fault.' It would be easier than having to pour out what's
inside me.

"Sometimes I want to tell Mom and Dad how I feel
about things, but I'm afraid they might think I'm talk-

ing back to them or trying to cause trouble, which is not what I want to do."

Jori would like to have a family that doesn't argue, when she grows up. "People can't be calm all the time, I know that. But I don't like shouting. If my kids are unhappy I hope they'll tell me what's bothering them or confide in their grandma, or a friend."

For Jori, the future now seems bright and full of promise. Her dreams are currently divided between becoming a nurse or a gymnast. Every Tuesday she takes gymnastic lessons, working hard to perfect forward handsprings from a vaulting horse. "I'm so full of energy and spirit when I'm practicing," she says. "I can go on forever. I love the feeling of being on top of the world."

"It's no joke when your father drinks, or used to"

MORGAN, age 7

Morgan was four years old when she learned her father was an alcoholic. "Mommy told my older sister, Jori, and me about Daddy's alcoholism. I was very young then and didn't know what she was talking about. But I knew something was wrong in my family. My parents argued too much," Morgan says.

At the same time, Morgan remembers having fun with her father, especially when he took her to work with him. "Daddy mostly drank at night or on weekends, but not when he had to go to work. Some days, if he wasn't too busy, I went with him. We would have tacos for lunch, because he knew I loved them—I still do."

Morgan recalls another time when her father took the family to the circus. "I had a great time because I knew Daddy wouldn't get drunk there. He didn't drink on holidays, either. When we had wine on Passover, he only sipped a little."

When Morgan's father had too much alcohol, though, he frightened her. "Mostly Daddy shouted at Mommy, but it still scared Jori and me. To get away from the noise, Jori pulled me with her into another room. Then we'd hold each other tightly and peek out to see what was happening. The worst thing I remember was when he threw a metal chair at Mommy. Luckily she ducked in time. In a second, Jori grabbed my hand, and together we raced out of the apartment, down the hallway to a friend's house. We stayed there until things got quiet."

Despite her father's drinking, Morgan invited friends to the house. Usually they visited in the afternoon when her father worked. "My friends and I played in my bedroom. When Daddy came home, I introduced everyone to him even if he was drunk. After all, he was my father. But he acted real weird then. He'd say, 'Take your friends outside, Morgan; I want to watch TV in the living room.' What's strange is that we weren't even near him. We played in *my* room. Drinking confused Daddy.

"And it made him forget his promises. When I was almost five, Daddy said that he would buy me a baton when he came home from work, because I had asked for one for so long. That night, he didn't come home at all, and I remember going to bed sad. What made it worse was that it wasn't the first time he forgot to bring me something. When he drank, his mind went blank. Something clogged it up."

Just before Morgan's fifth birthday, her father moved into his own apartment. He had secretly packed a suitcase during the day when no one was in the house. That evening he didn't come home from work. "Jori, Mommy, and I waited up till late, wondering where he could be. I kept asking Mommy, 'Is he here yet?' and she shook her head no. Then we noticed the missing radio. Mommy figured out that Daddy must have taken it, but we couldn't understand why.

"The next day he called to tell us where he was. I kept wondering, how could Daddy leave, when I loved him so much," Morgan says. "I was so sad that he'd forget about me, and I was frightened I'd never see him again."

That didn't happen, Morgan is pleased to say, convinced now that her father never stopped loving her all the time he lived away from home. When he first left, though, she wasn't sure of anything.

"Daddy and Mommy were apart for nine months. I wasn't even five then, but I worried about Daddy being by himself. Who would take care of him if something terrible happened? Before I was born, Daddy crashed a car into a tree and got hurt. If he had another accident, I thought, nobody would be there to help him get better. It's hard when a daddy drinks and moves out."

Although Morgan missed her father, she continued to be frightened when she visited him. "If I went to his apartment, I worried he might make me stay there forever because he was lonely. And when he came to our house to see Jori and me, he scared me when he lost his temper with Mommy. One time he yelled so much, I ran to our neighbor's in my pajamas. Daddy didn't like that and came after me. He tried to carry me home, but I cried so much he finally put me down. Later that night, he came to kiss me good-bye."

It was confusing having a father who shouted one minute, then hugged the next. "Who knew what was going on with him?" Morgan says. "That rotten whiskey caused so many problems."

Throughout the years her father drank, Morgan says she didn't talk much about it to anyone. "My grandparents knew about Daddy, but they never saw him drunk, so they couldn't understand what went on in our house. Besides, Daddy didn't want anyone to know about his problem. He said it would give people something to talk about."

The person she came to rely on most was her sister Jori. "I had to be hospitalized once with a broken nose, and Jori helped me feel better by talking softly to me. And whenever Daddy exploded, Jori knew what to do. I love her," she exclaims.

Once Jori began attending meetings at the treatment center, she shared what she learned with Morgan, who was too young to go. "I remember one time Jori brought home a coloring book that had stories about alcoholism. We drew in it together, while Jori explained the pictures to me. Although I couldn't understand a lot of what she told me, it still helped. My sister's so nice."

Morgan can't say exactly what made her father stop drinking altogether, but she thinks he missed the family after he moved out and knew he couldn't return unless he came back sober. "Anyway, three years ago he joined AA and decided not to touch another drop of whiskey again. He won't even eat chocolates that have liquor in the middle," Morgan says proudly.

When Morgan looks around at other families, she sees that in some ways hers resembles them. "We celebrate holidays together, and Jori and I get money from the tooth fairy. But I know that because of Daddy's alcoholism, my family is different. Even though Daddy stopped drinking three years ago, all of us still go to meetings. Daddy goes to AA, Mommy goes to Al-Anon, and Jori and I go to the treatment center."

At the center Morgan talks to other children who have alcoholic parents, and at home now she feels comfortable discussing her father's disease with her family. "It's much easier not having to keep Daddy's alcoholism a secret anymore. Sometimes friends wonder if I'm bored with the meetings since I've been going for so long, but I have fun at the center, and I like the kids there."

Morgan has told some of the children in her school that she attends meetings to help her understand her father's drinking problem. "Most kids don't know what

I'm talking about and a few laugh when I describe how Daddy acted. 'No parent does that,' some mean boys said to me. They didn't believe what I told them. Finally, I said, 'It's no joke when your father drinks, or used to. Be happy it's not your father.' "

On Tuesdays Morgan reminds her teacher that she's going to the treatment center that night so her homework won't be completed. Despite this explanation, for many weeks her teacher gave her a poor grade on the assignment. "I don't think she listened when I told her about Daddy's problem, or maybe she didn't understand. Finally, one day when I explained it for the hundredth time she said, 'Now I know.' Since then, she hasn't given me a bad mark. But it took so long.

"Many people think, 'So what's the big deal if your parent has a drinking problem?' They don't realize how hard it is for kids when a mommy or daddy gets drunk. I know that most parents don't drink, so their children don't worry about that kind of stuff. But a lot of parents *are* alcoholics. People should be more understanding and kinder when they're with those kids."

Since her father stopped drinking, Morgan says, she's no longer afraid of him. "Daddy yells less now, so I don't worry anymore how he'll act when I invite friends over." Even so, his alcoholism remains very much on her mind. "I know Daddy hasn't had whiskey in three years, but I still think about it a lot."

When Morgan gets older she says she won't drink or smoke. "Mommy used to smoke and Daddy, too, but they both stopped. Smoking and drinking can hurt you. I don't want to hurt myself."

Looking back, Morgan feels lucky her father went into recovery. "His drinking made too many problems for the family. Now it's so much better in our house. Still, I loved Daddy all the time, whether he drank or not. I'm glad he's my father."

"For a long time I wouldn't believe the truth"

KENDEL, age 12

"Until I was ten, I didn't realize Dad had a drinking problem or that my parents had trouble with their marriage. One night, though, I remember hearing Mom cry after she and Dad had a fight. It was about his alcoholism. That was the first time I heard that word mentioned in my house. Then Mom brought my sister, Katy, and me to a treatment center where the counselor told us our parents were getting a divorce because of my father's drinking. I said, 'Not my family!' I was sure we were normal. My parents hardly argued. For a long time I wouldn't believe the truth."

Now Kendel, ten-year-old Katy, and their mother live with their grandparents. Kendel's mother does not make enough money as a secretary to support the three of them in a place of their own. On weekends Kendel and Katy visit their father. Mostly, when they see him, they do chores together. "We'll shop for groceries or do jobs around the house. It gets boring sometimes, but I'm happy just being with Dad. I like the way he cooks, and we have fun gardening. Also, he has these cute dogs I play with."

Kendel's biggest fear when her father drinks is that he'll drive drunk and crash the car, harming himself and others. Whenever she enters a poster contest about alcoholism, her theme is that drunken driving can kill. "In fifth grade, my poster was so good, I almost won a trip to Disney World but not quite. Instead, I got a T-shirt," she says. "Dad's drunken driving is on my mind a lot. I don't know why he does it."

Recently Kendel discovered that alcoholism runs in her family. Her uncle on her mother's side drinks, and so did her mother's grandfather. On her father's side, Kendel's grandpa drinks, too. "Since the divorce Dad has lived with Grandpa," Kendel explains. "When we visit, Grandpa often brings home a six-pack from the grocery.

"For as long as I remember, Dad drank at home. But I never thought of him as an alcoholic. He didn't act violent, fall asleep after drinking, or throw up. In fact, I've never seen Dad drunk or even high. When he's had a lot of beer, he acts the same as he usually does."

A few years ago, after talking to their counselor at the treatment center, Kendel and her sister convinced their father to go with them to a meeting, hoping he would get involved in a program. After attending one session, he agreed to try nonalcoholic beer. "Dad drank that for one week but didn't like the taste and went right back to the alcoholic stuff. I was mad at him. He knew how much his drinking bothered Katy and me. But still I loved him."

After this experience with her father, Kendel had a different attitude toward her mother. Before, she blamed her mother for not convincing her father to give up alcohol. But now that she and Katy haven't been successful, either, she sees how difficult it is to change another person. "Maybe if Katy and I threatened not to see Dad again, he might quit—Dad says we're the most important people in his life. But I'm not ready to do anything that drastic. Besides, I like being with him. I feel badly when I miss a weekend at his house."

Sometimes, though, too much alcohol puts Kendel's father in a bad mood. "If Katy and I feel that we've had enough, we tell Dad how he ruined our time. It would be foolish if we kept these feelings to ourselves," Kendel says. "I know Dad cares about us because he apologizes and tries to comfort us by explaining that he's cut back on the amount of beer he drinks. He tells the truth, but he still drinks too much."

Most often, when she and her father are together, Kendel concentrates on making it a special time. "At Dad's house, I like pretending I'm the mother. In that way it's fun being the older daughter. I bake popovers for dinner and act as if I'm in charge of the kitchen. At home, Grandma mainly does the cooking."

Kendel thinks that if she is helpful her father will be more pleased with her. "I'm a good kid, and I'll do chores for Dad before he asks. Usually I volunteer for jobs no one else likes. While he prepares the barbecue, I set the table, and after dinner, I clear it. Since I know Dad likes a clean house, I keep after Katy to pick up her clothes and make her bed. Because Dad and I are so much alike, we get along well.

"Since my parents' divorce, Dad only seems happy when Katy and I visit," Kendel observes. "It's hard for him living by himself. Grandpa's usually not home, and when he is, Dad and he don't get along."

At times Kendel thinks about permanently living with her father; usually she feels this way when she has to leave him at the close of the weekend, or when she's had an argument with her mother. But so far, she hasn't made any definite plans.

"If my parents hadn't divorced, I wouldn't be thinking about Dad's loneliness. In the beginning, I was angriest at Mom for ending the marriage, but now I see she didn't have much choice as long as Dad drank. Mom says Dad was hurting the family and she had to do something to protect us."

Kendel became so concerned about her father that she debated whether or not to go to sleepaway camp this summer. "At first, I was looking forward to camp," she explains. "I had gone before and became real good at tennis and badminton. Then I started thinking how lonely Dad would be with Katy and me away for six weeks, so I persuaded Mom to let us stay with him the whole time instead. I can't wait to see Dad every day. It'll be such fun, even though I'm expecting more chores."

At this moment, Kendel sees no signs of her father controlling his drinking, yet she still has hope. "My friend Jori, at the treatment center, never thought her father would go into recovery, but he did. Maybe the same thing will happen to Dad," Kendel confides. "Mom and I talk about it, but there's not much she can tell me. And although Katy and I are close in age we don't mention our father's problem. It makes us feel too uncomfortable."

Kendel has discussed her father's drinking with her best friend, Nicola, who became curious when Kendel went to the treatment center each week. "Nicola asked what was going on, so I told her. All she said was, 'Oh.' Nothing more. I guess she didn't want to make a big deal of it. Since my other friends haven't asked, I haven't offered any information. When they come to my house, we'll play Hangman or other board games, but we usually don't talk about personal stuff."

Of all her friends, Kendel confides most in Jori, since they come from similar backgrounds. "Jori understands my feelings. Although her father no longer drinks, she still goes to meetings at the center. We're in the same group. If one of us is tired and would rather not go, she'll call the other one up, and we'll decide together. Usually we end up attending the meeting and feel better afterward. We might join Alateen soon," Kendel says, referring to the organization for teenagers with alcoholic parents.

Listening to Jori talk about her father gives Kendel hope. "Maybe Dad will recover someday, like Jori's father. I get jealous when she describes how much happier her family is now.

"When I'm older, I'm going to try not to marry an alcoholic. It makes things too complicated. If I have kids I'll make sure they get enough attention, although I'm certain I won't have a perfect family. Who does?

"At least I know about alcoholism and can teach my kids how bad it is. I'll also tell them not to try drugs or to smoke."

Kendel likes the idea of teaching children and might consider doing that when she gets older. "Since first grade I've thought about being a teacher," she says. "People say I talk softly and am kind, so I think kids will like me."

Postscript: Kendel and Katy spent only three weeks of their summer vacation with their father. Then he became seriously ill from the effects of alcoholism and had to be hospitalized. If he wanted to live, the doctors told him, he would have to go into rehabilitation and stop drinking forever. Kendel's father has said he would try.

As far as Kendel is aware, her father has not had a drink for two months. Since she's known him, that's the longest period she has seen him sober.

"More than anything, I didn't want to let my parents down"

KERRY, age 30

The youngest of three children, Kerry grew up in a home where drinking was standard behavior. Both his parents drank, as did each of his grandfathers. One of his uncles died from an alcohol-related disease, while another uncle and two aunts belong to AA. "Even my two older sisters drink too much, but they deny it," Kerry says. "In our house, drinking was part of every-day life. In the evening, when Dad came home from work, he and Mom talked and drank in the kitchen. At dinner, they drank more, usually finishing two bottles of wine a night. Then they'd have an after-dinner drink."

For most of his life, Kerry didn't realize his parents were alcoholics, nor did they. "As the children of alcoholics, Mom and Dad thought they behaved like most adults. Having grown up in alcoholic environments, they had no model for a normal home life. Finally, twelve years ago, they joined AA. That really surprised me. I didn't think of alcohol as the cause of the troubles in their marriage.

"Now that they've stopped drinking, they seem to get along much better. Next it's my turn to work on myself," Kerry admits.

In retrospect, Kerry realizes how angry and frustrated he was for much of his childhood. He wishes he had talked to someone who could have advised him to stop taking the blame for his parents' problems. "Maybe then I wouldn't have felt rotten so much of the time."

Although both of his parents drank heavily during his growing-up years, he had more difficulty getting along with his mother. It didn't help that she disapproved of his two hobbies: boxing and restoring motorcycles. Kerry tried to sway her opinion by appealing to his father for support. "Dad would sympathize with me, but in the end he'd side with Mom. If I mentioned either boxing or motorbikes when the two of them were around, Dad literally got behind Mom and signaled for me to be quiet. Finally, I gave up and went to my room, pouring out my feelings by punching a bag."

Still, Kerry kept trying to win over his mother. "I mowed the lawn, bought her candy, and was an exceptionally good student. I even had a job throughout high school and college. But that didn't satisfy her or Dad, either. They expected this kind of outstanding behavior and rarely praised me for it. In fact, Mom complained that I was away working too much so that I couldn't do the chores she had lined up for me at home."

When Kerry was thirteen, he became friends with Eddie, a schoolmate who had four brothers. "I missed a brother relationship and jumped at the chance of being close to a family with five boys. Besides, I liked Eddie's parents. They welcomed me into their house and didn't question why I never invited their son to my home. Eddie's mother, in particular, was understanding. She listened when I told her about Mom's lack of interest in my hobbies.

"With time, she and I became so close I called her Almost Mom. I liked Eddie's dad, too. He was a good guy. We played checkers together, and he kidded me in an affectionate way. In Eddie's family's mind, I was terrific. When I did well in school, they complimented me. When I told jokes, they laughed. But mostly, they liked me for being *me*."

Even though he had the support of Eddie's parents, Kerry still continued to work hard to earn his own mother's and father's approval. In eighth grade, at his father's suggestion, he took an entrance exam for a special high school. "Dad wanted me to be a doctor or lawyer and thought this test would improve my chances in either field. When I failed the exam, I felt awful, thinking I had disappointed him. More than anything, I didn't want to let my parents down," Kerry explains.

At the end of that school year, Kerry's report card showed a 99 percent for one final examination and 100 percent for all the others. "My teacher made a fuss over my marks, but I shrugged it off. By then so much of my life was geared to pleasing others, nothing I did felt satisfying. If I got an A on a test, I didn't take the time to pat myself on the back. I worried too much about how I would do on the next exam. When I played football on the high school team, I concentrated so much on being perfect that I couldn't loosen up and enjoy the game.

"I understand now how I beat up on myself, and how awful I honestly felt much of the time. Yet I also recognize that I had tremendous determination and willpower, which helped me survive. Still, I could have been much kinder to myself and had more fun," Kerry confesses.

After Kerry's parents joined AA, he started seeing positive changes in their behavior. When his mother had been in the program for eight years she encouraged him to join an ACOA group, and he agreed. "For three and a half years I've attended ACOA meetings," he says, "trying to understand how my parents' alcoholism affected me. Now I realize that I have many of the traits of a kid growing up in an alcoholic environment. Before that, I blamed myself for my family's problems, thinking that if I were perfect, everything would work out okay.

"But that's changed, I'm proud to say. ACOA and individual therapy have helped me think better of myself. Two years ago, I got the courage to leave a job I disliked. It was the first time I had taken a chance, and I was scared. When I applied to the company I had my heart set on, they offered me a low salary, which set me reeling. Thank goodness I mustered up enough courage to convince them I deserved more pay, and they agreed."

Thanks to ACOA's help, Kerry says he can talk to others about his parents' alcoholism. Although he feels close to his sister Karen, he confides most in other ACOA members. "Right now they're my best friends." The group has enabled Kerry to see how he's hurt himself through the years, and he's determined to end that kind of behavior. "I'm aware that I accomplish nothing by trying to please others. I have to satisfy myself first, or else I won't be happy. For the first time in my life I'm having fun. With patience and hope, I know I'll be taking advantage of more good stuff that lies ahead."

"I want people to think
I'm smart and terrific and
to be pleased with what I do"

TIM, age 12

For as long as Tim remembers, his father drank. Every night when his dad came home from his job, he'd turn on the television set and have one beer after another. "That was Dad," Tim says. "He'd drink, talk to me, help me with my homework, and then fall asleep in a chair. I didn't think anything was wrong with how he acted."

Two years ago, when Tim's mother told him she was divorcing his father because of his alcoholism, it surprised Tim. "Sure, my parents fought a lot, and I hated when they did that. But I couldn't understand the part about his drinking," Tim explains. "Why would my mother leave my father for that? His drinking didn't bother *me*."

Now Tim knows more about alcoholism and understands how his father's disease began to seem "normal."

"Alcoholism runs in my family. Not only Dad, but both my grandfathers are alcoholics. Mom's father only stopped drinking a few years ago after too much liquor made him seriously ill," Tim explains. Tim's mother, having grown up in an alcoholic home, hadn't seen anything unusual in her husband's drinking. "Only when Mom's friend convinced her to join Al-Anon did she understand what was happening to our family."

It didn't help either that his father's friends drank, too. "Whenever we'd go to someone's house, the women talked together on one side of the room, while the men drank and watched TV on the other. I stayed with the men and talked sports, never caring that they drank lots of beer or whiskey. That's how all men act, I thought.

"Anyway, Dad didn't behave like the alcoholics I read about in books or saw on TV. When he drank he wouldn't throw up, break furniture, fall down, or beat anybody. Mostly, he yelled or gave someone a shove. That's why it was hard for me to accept that Dad had a disease. Besides, I can remember so many good times we shared together," he says thoughtfully.

"Almost every Christmas, Mom, Dad, my younger brother, and I celebrated at home or visited friends who had kids, too. On Thanksgiving we went to my grandparents, and I saw my cousins, whom I like a lot. On holidays and on my birthday, I don't ever remember Dad being drunk."

Which is not to say there weren't bad times, too.

When Tim's father drank, his parents usually ended up in loud arguments. To get away from the screaming, Tim would play at a friend's house for as long as he could, or he'd bury himself in schoolwork. But he never talked to any adult about his home life. "How could I explain what was going on with my family, when I was so ashamed? It's not easy having a father who drinks."

Now Tim takes pride in his years of hard work at school. "I'm real smart," he boasts. "In class I don't read the same books as most kids and I take different math. I admit I put a lot of effort into what I do, but it pays off. Mostly I get A's in everything, but once I got a C in science—my worst subject. The teacher said I got a bad grade because I hadn't tried hard enough, but that's not true. I wanted to tell her off but didn't because I don't like to get into trouble."

Despite Tim's excellent performance in school, he thinks poorly of himself when he makes a mistake. Even a simple spelling error upsets him. "I get so embarrassed when that happens and can't believe how stupid I am. Nobody knows how I feel, though, because I put on a fake smile."

Recently Tim won a national award for inventing a new game in a Counting Dominoes Contest. He's also been on TV and has been written about in the newspaper. "I'm famous," he jokes. "Once a newspaper reporter interviewed me and asked what job I would *least* like to have. I answered, 'Being a hunter.' I'm not sure if that was a smart answer, but that's how I feel. I hope I didn't sound stupid.

"I want people to think I'm smart and terrific and to be pleased with what I do. I'm usually first to offer to run errands for teachers, bringing papers back and forth to the office. If anyone wants something done right, they always ask me first. Kids tease me for this, and I tell them off. But I like helping out."

At times, though, Tim finds that he says yes to people when he really means no. "If Mom does something that bothers me, I usually tell her. She's probably the only person I'm that honest with. But it's hard to be straight with other people who might yell back at me. I hate being yelled at, and I don't want to cause trouble, especially with Dad. If I talk back to him, he gets angry and scares me. When that happens, I immediately apologize, then get furious with myself for making him mad," Tim confides.

"In school, I haven't had the courage yet to say no to anyone. Imagine what the teacher would think!" Recently, instead of expressing his wish to play the drums rather than the cymbals, Tim quit the band altogether.

Today Tim lives with his mother and brother. Because of his father's drinking, the courts allow him and his brother to visit their dad only every other weekend. At times his dad has invited friends to the house to drink while Tim has been there. "That makes me mad," says Tim, "but I don't tell Dad how I feel. I just put on a fake smile and go to my room. I don't know what else to do," he adds, shrugging his shoulders.

Although Tim's father still drinks, Tim sees progress in the amount. "Now he only has a couple of beers a day—that's a little better than before. But he makes me sad because he won't stop completely. I don't know if he ever will.

"Sometimes I wonder what it would be like if Dad recovered from alcoholism. I know it wouldn't change my parents' marriage. That's over with—Mom told me. But if Dad stopped drinking, maybe the courts would agree to let him see my brother and me more often.

"I like Dad a lot and enjoy being with him, but I don't want to follow in his footsteps. He's caused too many problems with his drinking, and I never want to do that. I know for certain, I won't drink. Not me! Never!"

"I felt super-responsible
to rescue everyone"

RANJAN, age 36

"As far as I know, there's no history of alcoholism in my family. My father was the first to have a drinking problem. Even though I was seven when I realized he drank a lot, it's taken me a long time to accept the idea that he is an alcoholic."

Ranjan was born in India and lived there until he moved to the United States at age twenty to attend graduate school. America has been his home ever since. "I've felt lonely for most of my years in this country and have blamed that on being a foreigner, which in a way is true. But I must admit that I've felt apart from the group since I was five years old. That's when my father left our family for Bhilai, a city in northern India. As a mechanical engineer, he thought he'd have more opportunity for work there. Unfortunately, in the two years he lived away from us he became involved with alcohol," Ranjan explains.

Until age seven, Ranjan lived on his grandfather's farm, in the southern part of the country. "I used to run around the fields with my friends or take walks with Grandfather. I loved being with him. He treated me as a special child and affectionately answered all my questions.

"My mother, too, enjoyed living in the countryside near her mother. But once Dad left, everything changed. The first year he wrote to us, describing details of city life. The second year, his letters stopped, and I sensed Mom's concern.

"The next thing I knew, we were packing our belongings to join Dad, one thousand miles away from where I had grown up. Not only did I have to leave my relatives, I had to enroll in a new school and learn another language, Hindi."

Almost as soon as they arrived in Bhilai, Ranjan noticed his father's drinking. From that moment on, he says, his family life changed. "As the oldest of the children—my sister Rita is four years younger and Deepa, who wasn't born yet, is eleven years younger—I was more aware of what was happening at home. I didn't have them to talk to then, and even years later, the three of us wouldn't discuss Dad's alcoholism. The most we ever said about it to each other was, 'He drinks a lot.'

"Usually Dad drank before he came home, which was often late at night. While my parents hoped the children wouldn't know about their private life, they couldn't hide it. Through the thin walls, I heard Mom cry while Dad yelled. Much later my mother told me that Dad even hit her. While I never saw him violent, I believe her."

Over the years, Ranjan's father's salary went up and down. Sometimes the family had a spacious home with their own chauffeur, while at other times they lived in a converted garage apartment.

Although Ranjan and his father had some good times together, "Mostly Dad acted harsh with me. When he was around, I kept my radar up. As a young child, I played quietly by myself, and then in later years I buried myself in schoolwork. Since I loved math especially, I didn't mind reading it for hours. However cramped our apartment, I managed to find a small section of the house in which to study. During my teenage years I went to the school library on weekends as an excuse to get away from the chaos. There, I found peace in math books. School was my salvation. It helped me forget about Dad's drinking—for a while. Besides, I thought my studying pleased Dad, who pushed us children to learn."

Still, Ranjan says, his father often found fault with whatever he did or said. "If I told him I wanted to be a scientist, he said that was too intellectual, and I should become an engineer. When I asked him for money to buy schoolbooks, he said we didn't have funds, but ten minutes later he would send me out to buy liquor. He was a powerful father, and I was afraid of him."

Even after years of continuous turmoil in his house, Ranjan still didn't realize how different his family was from most or consider his problems unusual. "Indians in particular accept suffering as part of life's struggle, so while Dad's drinking frustrated and angered me, I said nothing but felt terrible inside," Ranjan confesses.

Nor did Ranjan speak to anyone about his family. "In India, it's not socially acceptable to tell outsiders about your private life. Instead, I kept my thoughts to myself." Although he made friends easily, he avoided their curiosity by not inviting them to his home.

When Ranjan was in his early teens, his father imposed isolation on the entire family. "Dad wouldn't permit anyone to come to our house. We no longer celebrated holidays. On Christmas, Mom baked cakes, but that was all, and on the Hindu festivals, Dad gave me money to buy fireworks to set off with my friends, though no celebration went on at home.

"Soon we stopped eating meals together. Dad wanted to be on his own, so we ate without him. Besides, when he came home, he acted as if he were in another world."

About this time, Ranjan's father also forbade the family to have any further contact with their relatives. "Since Indian husbands set the rules at home, Mom obeyed. As an obedient wife, Mom stopped writing to her family and no longer visited them. She didn't even know when her parents died."

With no other family or friends to talk to, Ranjan's mother began to confide in her children. "As the oldest, I was the one she leaned on the most," he says. "On the one hand, I felt flattered that my mother shared her thoughts with me and asked for my support. On the other hand, I was angry with her for burdening me, a child.

"What was worse, Mom emphasized that if something happened to Dad I had the obligation as the first son to take care of the family. In India, that's not an unreasonable request, but with my alcoholic father, I felt super-responsible to rescue everyone."

Ranjan began to believe that only he could fix his family's problems. "Whenever Mom asked me to do a favor, I always complied. At seventeen, I took typing, which didn't particularly interest me, but I thought it might help me get a job more easily, in case I had to support the family. Two years before, Dad had suffered a heart attack, and I had been afraid we'd run out of money."

Looking back, Ranjan believes he was given adult responsibilities too early in life. "I've worked hard since I was a child, thinking that was the only way to rescue the family. Work and friends have filled my days for as long as I can remember. They helped me keep my mind off my problems. But I see now that if I had dealt with my problems differently, I could have enjoyed myself more through the years. The only time I remember being particularly excited about anything was when I came in first in all of India in the National Science Contest." Ranjan beams. "I was seventeen then."

However, Ranjan says, his hard work, determination, and persistence paid off for him in many ways. "It enabled me to get out of my chaotic house sooner than I had expected and to go to America. Because of my high grades throughout my school years, for instance, I had no trouble getting good-paying jobs. Today I'm fortunate enough to earn sufficient money to take care of my physical needs and have extra for my personal life.

"I just wish that, as a child, I had had the knowledge of alcoholism I have now. Then I would have found ways to feel less isolated."

Only lately has Ranjan begun to give up his impossible dream of saving his family. "After years of offering half my salary to my sisters so they could attend graduate school, I stopped. In India, it's not uncommon for older brothers to help out, but my sisters, like my parents, wouldn't help themselves. The more money I sent them, the more they asked for."

As recently as two years ago, Ranjan suggested his parents move to America. He hoped that if they lived near him, he could convince his father to seek treatment. "When Dad wouldn't consider my offer, I gave up trying to change him," he says.

Ranjan does not regret taking care of his family, but he now understands that it's important to take care of himself as well. "In India, the family comes first, before your own needs. After being in ACOA and talking to a therapist, I now believe that if I feel good about myself, my family situation will work out."

No longer embarrassed for others to see how sparsely decorated his home is, Ranjan has begun inviting people to visit him there. "Suddenly I realized I was still secluding myself, just as I had as a child. I'm glad I'm finally beginning to change. I see things are working out for me."

In a few years, Ranjan hopes to get married and raise a family. "I have a lot of positive qualities." He smiles teasingly. "I'm pleasant, nice looking, and have a good job.

"But most important, I'm patient, and I have hope. That's been the key to my success throughout my life."

"I never knew
what to expect from
one day to the next"

JOHN, age 11

"John's my dad's name, not mine. I use it since I like
him a lot and sometimes think about being him. But I
wouldn't want to be Dad one hundred percent. Dad's
messed up too much with his drinking. I know I'll
never drink. That I'm sure of."

In John's memories, drinking was always a part of his
father's life. But not until John was seven years old and
his parents divorced did he learn his father was an alcoholic. "Before that I knew something was wrong with
my family. I just didn't know what it was.

"Once, I was asleep when Dad came home from a
trip to California. I woke up when I heard him and
Mom yelling at each other. When I asked what was
wrong, Mom said I must have had a nightmare. I was
only six, but I didn't believe her."

Other times, John's father drank and stayed away

from home for days. That, more than anything else, frightened John, who worried he might not see his father again. "I used to cry when he didn't show up. Jacqueline, my older sister, tried to make me feel better by saying everything would be okay. Then she'd start crying, too. Eventually Dad would come home, and for a while things would be fine. He'd stop drinking and act real nice. If we played catch he'd put his arm around me and tell me how good I was. Some days, he'd take me to work with him. I loved that.

"Then all of a sudden, he'd start drinking again. Dad's drinking went in streaks. He'd stop and start, stop and start. I never knew what to expect from one day to the next."

Looking back, John realizes how alone he felt at these times, even with his mother at home. "Mom was too worried about Dad to pay attention to me or my sister," John explains. "If Dad didn't come home on time, she'd stay up late making calls to places she thought he might be. When she couldn't find him, she'd phone her friends and cry. By the time Dad came home at night, drunk, of course, she'd be angry. Then they'd start fighting again."

Whenever John asked his mother why she and his father argued so much, she avoided answering him. "I was confused," John says. "Most of the time, I was angrier with Mom than Dad. I think I secretly blamed her for Dad's drinking. I thought that if she ignored it, instead of always talking about it, he would stop."

Now John knows his mother couldn't change his father. "You can't make someone stop drinking. But maybe Mom could have been more patient with me and answered my questions.

"Dad's drinking made everybody miserable, and nothing we did got him to quit. Mom and he tried going to AA meetings together, but that lasted only a short time. Then he went back to his old pattern," John recalls.

When sober, John's father promised to take him to restaurants as a treat. "He told me, 'Be ready to go out to eat as soon as I get home from work,' so I'd stop playing early and wait for him, all excited. When he came home, he'd be drunk, having forgotten the plans. And sometimes he wouldn't show up at all. I remember I'd sit for hours, watching the door, trying hard not to give up hope. Just thinking about it today makes me mad."

By the time John entered kindergarten, he was a very angry boy. He physically attacked any child who bothered him. "I even started fires on the school bus," he admits. "What a reputation I had. Regular teachers couldn't control me, so I was put into a class for difficult kids.

"Actually, that was the best thing that could have happened, since the teacher there appreciated me and said, 'Nice going,' or something like that, when I worked well. He made me feel great!"

Today John rarely gets into trouble at school.

"Almost immediately after Dad moved out, there was less tension at home. I missed him, but I also felt better. At the same time, I started going to a treatment center where people understand what alcoholism does to a family.

"When the counselor there first told me Dad was an alcoholic, I closed my ears. I didn't want to think about my father that way. For a long time, I wouldn't discuss his problem with anyone but the counselor because it hurt too much. Now my best friends, Jason and Michael, know about Dad. I told them the truth when they asked why my parents got divorced. All they said was, 'Oh.' I'm glad I have friends I can trust."

For two years now, John's father has been sober. And to John's surprise, he and his father have become friends.

John's not sure what actually made his father give up alcohol; he thinks his father's new wife might have helped. "When Dad remarried, his wife encouraged him to stop drinking. At the same time, his business improved. When I ask Dad why he stopped, he says he made up his mind to do it, and that was that. I wish he hadn't waited to change until Mom and he got divorced. Maybe we'd still be a family. It's too bad some things don't work out the way you want."

Not too long ago, John's father told him that alcoholism runs in their family, so John should be extra careful to avoid it. "Since Dad stopped drinking, he's been honest with me. He answers my questions truthfully, even when it makes him look bad. But when Dad drank, nobody else seemed to matter. He used to take me to the bar with him when he knew I disliked going. While he had beer with his friends, I played video games. I'd ask impatiently, 'Can we go home now?' and he'd say, 'Soon,' then he'd give me money for a Coke. I never told Dad how that upset me. Even now it's hard to be open with him," John admits.

Today, John visits his father on weekends or during the week and shares with him problems he's having in school or with his mother and sister. "I feel comfortable talking about those subjects with Dad because he helps me feel better. But I have to carefully choose what I discuss with him. I want Dad to be happy and not angry with me," John confesses. "Imagine if he had an accident because of something I said. Or what if he refused to see me? I can't take a chance on that."

Still, John says he and his father have a good relationship. "Dad's not strict, and he compliments me when I do a good job. Anyway, I think it's easier for people to get along with each other when they don't live together."

John has learned that although he can't do much to change his father, he can do many things to please himself. Last year in school, he was elected to the student council, and this semester his report card was his finest. "Nobody believed how well I did, especially me," he boasts. "I didn't even work that hard. Picture it if I really tried."

And John admits to having more fun with his friends, riding bikes and skateboarding together. But most of all, he likes eating dinner at his father's house and going to ball games with him. "We see each other more than we ever did before. It's wonderful, especially when Dad takes me to work with him. I love when he teaches me about the fire extinguishers he sells. If I have a son, I'll take him to work with me, too, and play ball with him the way Dad does with me. But I'll never drink. That way I won't be like Dad. I've finally learned how to feel good, and I don't want that to change."

"I wanted to punish them more than help myself"

BILL, age 45

For the first ten years of his life, Bill and his mother lived in his grandparents' home. Bill's parents were divorced when he was quite young.

"I hardly remember my father," Bill says. "However, many years after the divorce, Mom told me he had a drinking problem."

Bill's grandfather drank, too, but Bill did not recognize it. "No one in my family talked directly about Grandpa's drinking, so I assumed it was normal for guys to go to a bar after working all day."

And although Bill overheard arguments between his grandparents, his grandfather usually acted loving and kind to him. "In many ways," Bill recalls, "Grandpa was like a father and friend to me. We went to ball games together and fished or played cards."

All this ended when Bill's mother remarried. "The

minute I met my stepfather, I didn't like him. Something told me to watch out. Soon, his problems became obvious. He was an alcoholic, too. And not only did he drink, but he beat Mom, and me as well.

"Mom had two children with Dad—I called him Dad from the beginning—and in his eyes, my stepbrothers were angels, while I was a troublemaker. When they got gifts, I got beatings. There was rarely a moment I could relax. Even when I played with my friends after school, I had to keep looking at my watch to make sure I got home before sundown, otherwise I'd be hit.

"No matter how I tried to please Dad, it didn't work. He kept looking for ways to start fights. Once I painted the hallway ceiling, thinking he'd compliment me, but he didn't even notice. When Mom said to him, 'Look what Billy did,' Dad just pointed out the spots I had missed.

"Despite my mother's efforts to protect me, nothing spared me from Dad's anger. Even when she lied to save me, I still got hit. When Dad drank, he was determined to blame me for some incident, whether or not I had done anything wrong."

It amazes Bill that his mother stayed with his stepfather. "I used to pray she'd have the courage to get us both out of the house, but she never did. Once in a while, after a real bad fight, we'd visit my aunts. I'd hear Mom tell her sisters about the nightmare we were living. Although they'd urge her to end the marriage, she didn't."

Bill begged his mother many times to leave with him. When she asked, "Where're we gonna go?" he suggested to his uncle Jackie's. But she said no. "Mom was afraid. She never worked or had a driver's license. I guess it was easier for her to depend on others," Bill says sadly. "Still, when I think about it now, it makes me angry. For years she never stopped Dad from hurting the family. On weekends, for instance, we went in the car with him while he drove drunk. I was terrified, and so was Mom. But the more she told him to slow down, the faster Dad drove. Soon I knew I had to protect myself."

After being repeatedly locked out of the house and hit for no reason, Bill became so desperate that he ran away from home. "I had just started high school. But I was so angry with my parents that I wanted to punish them more than help myself. I thought, 'Wait until they see what it's like not having me around.'

"In the end, I paid a big price for that type of thinking. At fourteen years old, I gave up my childhood. From the moment I left home, I had to become an adult and take care of myself," Bill explains. And he was extraordinarily lucky to have survived.

Looking back, Bill wishes he had trusted other people more and confided in them. "I'm sure my uncle Jackie would have helped me. But I was afraid to show anyone my feelings. Instead, I acted like a tough kid, who could take charge of anything. But in fact, I was very naive and innocent."

Away from home, Bill attended school and worked as a messenger to help support himself. "At no time did I ever consider quitting school. I was determined to graduate and get a good job."

At work, he became friends with a retired sixty-five-year-old boxing coach named Frank who was a messenger, too. Bill describes Frank as a gentle person with a sense of humor. "Almost immediately I knew I could trust him," he says, "and over time I told him about my past. I couldn't share everything. Some of the details embarrassed me and were too unbelievable. I worried that Frank might think I made them up."

For several years, Bill thought of Frank as the father he never had. "He took me to get a social security number, and showed me how to file tax reports. But mostly he cared about me. Whenever I try to be a better father to my own children, I remember Frank."

Bill spent all of his high school years away from home. For a time he stayed with his friend Dennis and his family, which, he says, gave him the experience of being in a stable home. "Dennis's family was warm to me," Bill explains, "and living with them helped me save money."

While not a great student—Bill mostly did his homework on the subway ride to school—he passed all of his subjects, even earning 90s in math. "For some reason, math came like a piece of cake. I hardly studied, yet I got A's. When I look back, I can't believe how much determination I had. And I'm grateful for it because if

I hadn't stayed in school, I wouldn't have the good job I have today."

While living with Dennis's family, Bill's biological father contacted him. "Dennis's dad arranged it. He thought it was for my own good. But after not seeing my father for so long, he seemed like a stranger to me, and his new wife was a stranger, too. Although they treated me nicely, I felt out of place. So when my father asked me to live with him, I refused. A few months later, however, I changed my mind. Dennis began having problems with his parents, and not wanting to be in the way, I accepted my father's offer. Oddly, I blamed myself for the troubles in Dennis's house, just as I secretly believed I caused my stepfather's drinking. In each situation I thought I'd better leave."

Even as an adult, Bill says, he has to fight the urge to run away when something goes wrong. "At home and at work, too, I often fight an internal war. My feelings say, 'Run away fast,' but my logic reminds me that I'm no longer a kid, getting hit for being a bad boy."

Two years ago Bill joined an ACOA group, which has finally helped him to understand how alcoholism has affected his life. "I used to be afraid of the night because I associated it with my stepfather's drunken behavior, and holidays depressed me, too, because Dad drank a lot then and made me miserable. Now I actually relax and enjoy the holidays and even look forward to them."

Today Bill believes that many positive qualities in his

personality surfaced because of his chaotic childhood. "I'm a survivor, which probably helped me most living with an alcoholic parent. And I'm a hard worker, too." He is most proud, however, of his ability to communicate with all types of people. "I'm comfortable speaking with the cleaning person as well as the chairman of the board. And I particularly appreciate the problems of the poor, since I lived most of my high school years on very little money.

"In my mind every person is important and deserves respect. Nobody should be put down, not even my stepfather. Dad and I actually get along better today than we ever did. Now that he's in poor health, he hardly drinks and he acts mellower."

Learning about alcoholism as a disease has also given Bill a better perspective on himself and his family. Although he is not an alcoholic, his seventeen-year-old son drank and took drugs but is now in recovery.

Perhaps the biggest change in Bill's life is his willingness to trust other people. "In the past, I'd open the door a little, then quickly close it, so no one would know how I really felt. Now I keep a wedge there that allows people into my life, and I'm feeling better for it. I'm determined to keep it that way, opening the door wider and wider until I no longer struggle with the wish to run away."

"If someone says Mom shouldn't take care of us, then who will?"

ALEX, age 7

"A few months ago, my mom stopped drinking. She was in rehab for two weeks, then came out and joined AA for a while. Mom drank before I was born, and Dad did, too. A year and a half ago, my father died in a car accident. His friend John drove drunk, and he and Dad were killed." Alex says that if his father and John hadn't had so much alcohol, they might still be alive.

"When Mom told me about Dad's accident, I realized she might get hurt next, because she also drank a lot."

Alex says he never tried to stop his father from drinking. "I was too smart, knowing Dad would hit me if I told him what to do. Mom would hit me, also."

Once Alex's mother gave up drinking, Alex thought the hitting would stop, too, but that didn't happen. "What's different now is she brings my little sister, Andrea, and me to the alcohol treatment center right after we get hurt, so we can talk to someone," Alex explains. "Before I started going to the treatment center, I never told anybody about my family, not even Aunt Ruth, and I like her best of my relatives. I didn't understand what was going on when Dad hit Mom, and Mom hit Andrea and me. Since Mom also called me bad names, I thought I must be a terrible child. My counselor said that wasn't true and explained alcoholism to me. She said it's a disease that can make people angry and yell at each other."

Although Alex feels better now talking about his problems, he worries that if he shares the details of his home life, Andrea and he might be taken away from their mother. "If someone says Mom shouldn't take care of us, then who will?" is the thought that most worries Alex. Despite Alex's understanding of alcohol, he still wonders why his mother would want to hurt her children. "Andrea's so cute and little, and I'm a good kid."

When Alex's father was alive, his parents' drinking sometimes meant that he and Andrea were totally ignored. While his mother and father argued in front of the TV, Alex would do his best to care for Andrea. Their supper, when he was five years old and Andrea two, was raisin bran cereal. "That's all I could make then, but at least we had food. After we ate, I'd put Andrea to bed, usually with a messy diaper. My sister smelled awful, which made me feel bad. But what else could I do?"

When his parents' drinking got out of control, Alex took Andrea into his room and put her to bed in a sleeping bag next to him. "First I made sure Andrea was quiet, then I locked the bedroom door from the inside and hid the key in my dresser drawer, so Mom or Dad couldn't come in. Mom kept asking me to slip the key under the door, but I pretended to be asleep. If I gave in, I was afraid she might hit us."

Even today, Alex still takes care of Andrea, comforting her when she needs it. "She likes when I pat her and say, 'It's okay. It's okay.' When Dad died she stayed close to me day and night, and we both cried. Andrea knows she can count on me for protection. If I can help it, I won't let her get hurt."

Although his parents' drinking has given Alex many negative experiences, he quickly recalls the good times, too.

"When Dad was sober, he'd say, 'Alex, how'd you like to go for ice cream together?' Or he'd suggest we play catch. Baseball is one of my favorite sports. After school, my friend Joey and I play together, and Dad used to play with us, too. I liked those days best. Mom cooked supper and took care of Andrea while Dad, Joey, and I threw the ball back and forth to each other.

"Sometimes, though," he adds, "Dad drank during the game. He'd sit with a beer in one hand, while he threw the ball with the other. It was better than not having him there at all, but his drinking made me mad."

Anger is something Alex has a hard time expressing. He has been known to pick fights with the children in his class. And last month he threw a rock at the school bus. "I really wanted to hit a boy who made fun of me, but I decided that wouldn't be a good idea. So I tossed the rock hard and broke a window. Mom had to pay for it and wasn't happy."

Since his mother has been sober, Alex has noticed some improvements in her life. She lost weight, has a boyfriend who does not drink, and generally seems happier. While Alex is more hopeful about his family life now, he says that from time to time, his mother still takes a drink. "When we don't have enough money because Mom's going to school and not working, she worries and so do I. It frightens me to see her drink again, and I want her to stop; so does her boyfriend. I think she might do it because she's happier when she's away from it." Although Alex realizes he can't do anything to change his family situation, it still frustrates him. "Maybe if I had taken better care of Dad, he might be alive today."

As for his own future, Alex has his sights set on becoming a fireman. "Then I can help people, and that's important. Helping people is what I do best."

"Nobody knew how frightened I was"

LYNN, age 40

"Both my parents were alcoholics and came from alcoholic families, even though they denied it. When my mother was ten years old she had her first drink. Her father offered her beer with dinner and afterward, too. Despite that, Mom didn't become a real drinker until she was my age.

"Of my two parents, Dad drank the most and for the longest time. He died sixteen years ago as a result of drinking, smoking, and heart disease. Mom died fourteen years later," Lynn says.

At age nine, Lynn became aware of her parents' drinking problem, although she suspects her father drank even before he got married. "For a long time I had uncomfortable feelings about my parents' use of alcohol, but I couldn't explain what bothered me. Whenever they had a party, the two of them ended the evening sick and complained of headaches the following morning."

When her father's job forced the family to move to another city, however, the drinking occurred more often. "Dad had to travel a lot, which made him and Mom unhappy. And Mom, who couldn't drive, had to depend on neighbors to take her everywhere.

"So on weekends and sometimes during the week, she and Dad relaxed with a few drinks. At first Mom drank to keep him company, but soon she began drinking heavily. It wasn't long before neither of them was available to me or my four sisters."

Lynn, the oldest of the children, tried to control the amount of alcohol her parents consumed. "When they passed out on Saturday nights I sneaked downstairs and poured out the rest of their liquor. That way we could have a sober Sunday. I knew the stores were closed then. During the week, I diluted their alcohol supply with water. But they caught on.

"Meanwhile, I couldn't understand what was happening in my family. Dad yelled at Mom over the least little thing. If she refused to argue with him, he'd turn against me. 'You can't do anything right,' he'd say. 'All the troubles in this family started the day you were born.'"

Although Lynn has fond memories of her mother playing with her, once the heavy drinking started, that stopped. "She made dinner and left it on the stove while she and Dad drank together," Lynn recalls. "In case we got hungry but didn't want to face Mom and Dad in the kitchen, we girls kept a reserve supply of popcorn upstairs.

"Other nights, we gobbled our supper before Dad came home. I ate so fast, then, I often choked. 'I'll fix them. I'll get ulcers, and they'll be sorry,' I remember thinking."

In all of this turmoil, Lynn felt responsible for protecting the family. "Too many things were going wrong and needed watching," she admits. "One night Dad fell asleep with a cigarette and burned the bedding. I smelled smoke and woke Mom up. If not for me, we might have lost our house.

"I became the prime caretaker, and my sister Karen, the second oldest, helped, too. While I mowed the lawn, tidied up the rooms, and vacuumed, she learned how to cook. Later, when I got my license, I drove the kids to their activities.

"Karen and I became inseparable. We held the family together. One Christmas Eve, when Dad and Mom passed out, we rummaged through the house trying to find the gifts so the little ones wouldn't be disappointed. The next day we took turns playing Santa Claus.

"Soon, everyone knew they could rely on me. If one of my sisters had a problem, I gave her emotional support. My baby sister Jocelyn, who's ten years younger than I, thinks of me as her mother more than our own mom. I practically raised her."

Throughout this time, Lynn blamed herself for her parents' drinking. She thought that if she could make them love her enough, she might be able to convince them to change their lives. "I swept the driveway and washed the laundry. When I left for school in the morning, I wore freshly cleaned and ironed clothes, even ironed underwear," she admits. "I didn't want anyone—especially my parents—to find fault with me.

"Lots of people saw me as very capable. Whenever someone in the neighborhood needed a baby-sitter, they called me first. But nobody knew how frightened I was." In school, Lynn sat quietly, hoping the teacher wouldn't call on her and find out what she didn't know. When she ice-skated in her free time, she assumed falls meant she needed to perfect her footing immediately. "I never gave in, not even when I felt exhaustion or pain. I was determined nobody would think I was lazy."

Looking back, Lynn sees that she worked especially hard to gain her father's love and attention. "I kept trying one way or another. Once, I remember asking him to help me improve in tennis, because I knew how much he liked that sport. He took me to the school yard and had me hit the balls against the wall while he sat down. 'Don't stop until I tell you,' he ordered."

But nothing Lynn did could make him happy. "Dad had too many problems," she says. "I realize now that I couldn't change him."

When she was in high school, Lynn finally told a friend about her problems at home. "I had known

Carol since the third grade, and I trusted her. She was the only person I invited to my house. I was too embarrassed to ask my other friends. Carol was always polite to my parents, whether or not they were drinking.

"During my senior year a girl named Judy moved to my town. Her mother was a falling-down drunk, and Judy, too, was the oldest of five children. We used to compare our family situations. I admitted my parents drank a lot, but I still didn't think of them as alcoholics. I reserved that term for bums I saw lying in the street."

Other than those two girls, Lynn didn't talk to anyone about her home life. No adult knew about her problems until a few years ago, when she went to a therapist and later joined an ACOA program.

Lynn regrets that neither of her parents went to AA or tried to change their lives. By the time her father realized how he had harmed himself with alcohol, it was too late; he never lived to see his grandchild, Lynn's sister's baby. Although her mother stopped drinking when Lynn's father died, she never joined AA or any other treatment program.

"I'm thankful I had the sense to get into the ACOA program. No matter what the weather, I go to meetings. The group helps me deal better with my feelings about my parents' disease. I finally believe that I didn't cause their alcoholism—that their drinking was not my fault."

If she had her childhood years to live over again, Lynn wishes that somebody would have helped her to realize how little she took care of herself. "If only someone could have pointed out what I was doing. Then maybe I wouldn't have hurt myself so much and could have dealt better with my alcoholic parents."

Her past, however, has not dampened her enthusiasm for life. "What most people take for granted, I now cherish—a balloon floating in the air, a crocus popping up in the spring. And somehow, too, I have developed love and compassion for people. But most important, for the first time in my life, I am optimistic about the future."

"I like being alone
at the controls"

SHAWN, age 8

"Since Mom thinks it's important I know about my family history, she told me that she and Dad drank and took drugs in high school. Although she stopped taking both when she was twenty-two, Dad only quit drugs. He's tried to give up drinking lots of times but goes right back to it again."

Now it's been seven months since Shawn's father's had a drink, the longest period he's stayed away from alcohol. "I'm not sure if he can keep it up," Shawn confides. "You'd think he'd want to, though, because he's so much calmer when he's sober, and it looks like he enjoys being with the family. Ever since Dad stopped drinking, he spends more time with me than ever before."

Until this year, however, Shawn says his father would come home from work every day, turn on the television, and drink one six-pack of beer after another. "Dad always seemed out of it, as if he were in another world. My brother, Jacob, and I would play right at his feet, but he never noticed if we were there or not."

Alcohol also made Shawn's father argumentative. "I was too young to understand that alcohol made Dad angry. I thought he yelled because he didn't like me. Even if I talked quietly to him he got upset, so I stayed out of his way or did whatever he asked without complaining. Dad scared me, but I wouldn't let him know," Shawn whispers.

If his father took Shawn with him to buy beer, Shawn kept it a secret from his mother. "I knew he shouldn't be sneaking six-packs, but I also wanted to be his friend, so I stayed silent. Besides, when Dad bought beer, I got a soda, so how could I tell on him? In a way it was fun . . . but confusing, too."

Many nights Shawn woke up and heard his parents shouting: his mother complaining about his father's drinking at bars and his father threatening her with divorce. "I didn't know whether or not to believe him, so I tried not to cry. But I was a little nervous. On weekends, if the fighting got real bad, Mom took us away for the day. It was great getting out of the house, but when I came home, I felt like crying."

Although Shawn's family lived in the downstairs part of his grandmother's house, he didn't share his feelings with her. "Grandma knew what was going on, but we never talked about it. When I visited her, I wouldn't tell her anything. I didn't say a word to my friends, either."

When Shawn was five and a half, his parents separated. For more than one year, his father lived away from home while the rest of the family continued living with Shawn's grandmother.

At the same time, Shawn started going to an alcohol treatment center to talk to other children with similar problems. "My counselor, Ellen, and some kids in the group explained to me that Dad was an alcoholic, which I never knew before. I always thought my father was angry because he didn't like me. The best thing was finding out that his drinking wasn't my fault, although it took a long time for me to believe it," Shawn says.

"I have a friend, Jake, who goes to my school and whose parents are divorced because his father also drank too much. We talk a lot about our dads. Before I went to the treatment center, I wouldn't tell anyone about my family, but now I feel comfortable telling my good friends."

During his parents' separation, Shawn's father was detoxified four times. "Each time Dad got detoxified, he stopped drinking for a few months, then he started all over again. It was crazy.

"One Christmas when I was almost seven, I wanted to visit him in the hospital, but he said he didn't want the family to see how awful he looked. I felt so sad and kept begging Mom to take me. Finally Dad agreed to let us come the following week. When he opened his presents then, he cried."

Nine months later, Shawn's father promised to stop drinking and to keep his word this time. "I think he missed the family too much and knew Mom wouldn't let him come back home unless he stayed sober.

"Four months after his last drink he came home. Sometimes Dad tells me he'd love a beer, but fights the urge. I know it's hard for him to quit forever, but he's trying. Every week he talks to a pastor who makes him feel better. Mom joined Al-Anon when he was away, and she wants him to join AA, but so far he hasn't."

Recently Shawn has been telling his father how sad and frightened he made him when he drank. He also asks his dad why he started drinking in the first place. "Dad explained that both his parents and his brother are alcoholics, and his two sisters took drugs. From the time he was a child, alcohol and drugs were part of his home life. As a teenager he thought using them was the grown-up thing to do. Then he met Mom, and they drank and took drugs together.

"When some of Dad's friends died from drugs, he got scared and stopped using them," Shawn says. "Maybe now he's finished with alcohol, too. If he goes back to it, he might die, and that worries me."

Now that his father doesn't drink, Shawn says the frightening arguments have stopped, but there are more rules in the house. "We eat health food, and we watch less TV." Sometimes Shawn balks, but he concedes, "It's worth it if Dad stays sober." Most important, Shawn says, the family spends more time together.

"Dad and I bought ten-speed bikes and ride side by side for five miles on a small road near the house. Or we take walks and talk. On Sundays the whole family goes to a large park where my younger sister, Rachel, my brother, Jacob, and I run around. When I think about it, I spend a lot of time with Dad. Many kids I know don't do that."

Looking toward the future, Shawn says he doesn't think he'll drink when he gets older. "It interferes too much with the family and causes too many problems. Sometimes I imagine what will happen to me, because so many people in my family had drinking and drug problems. And I wonder how I will act if my friends drink. That could be hard.

"My counselor, Ellen, says I'm in charge of my life. I'm the one to decide. I think about that a lot. On days when I have nobody to play with, I like to draw airplanes. I'm always the pilot, driving the plane. I like being alone at the controls. It's fun being in charge."

"For me, the best part of life has just started"

SARAH, age 25

"My dad was handsome, lovable, fun, and had a lot going for him," Sarah recalls. "With my older brother, sister, and me, he was wonderful. We had great times together. But Dad didn't know how to handle pressure.

"By the time I was six, he had a graduate degree in economics, a good job as a business consultant, and was attending school to get another degree in history." Her mother, a nurse, worked the night shift, while her father juggled a job and school. "It got to be too much for him."

Just when her father was about to receive his second graduate degree, he stopped school to take care of an alcoholic friend he had invited to live with the family. "That started Dad's pattern of quitting when life got hard. At this same time he also began coming home late from weekly office parties, bragging about the enormous pyramid he helped make with empty beer cans. Then he and Mom would fight."

Soon Sarah's father was openly drinking in front of the children or going to a bar and returning home drunk. "Dad's personality changed so much. It's hard to believe he was the same father. In the beginning, liquor relaxed him. It's funny, but I liked him better drunk, when he joked around, than when he was sober and irritable.

"But as he drank more and more, every little thing upset him, whether he was sober or drunk. If I turned the TV channels too fast, he'd scream. If I stood in front of the refrigerator with the door open too long, he'd yell. I quickly learned that to keep the peace, I had to be on constant guard.

"Although no one in my family ever admitted Dad was an alcoholic, I silently acknowledged it by the time I was eight. I'd hear Mom argue with Dad—about leaving the kitchen cabinet open or about having to clean up his beer cans. But she never addressed what really bothered her, his drinking."

Once her father was fired from his job (his drinking meant he could never arrive at work on time), Sarah's mother became the main wage earner of the family. Although her father worked off and on, his income was never steady, and he mostly spent it on liquor.

"When I was younger," Sarah recalls, "we owned a lovely house. Later, after Dad lost his job, we rented a house, instead. When that became too expensive, we moved to an apartment. Then we couldn't afford the rent there, so we moved to a less expensive apartment.

"Once, Mom picked me up from school and said we were going to Michigan to visit my grandparents. In reality, we had been evicted from our home, but she didn't have the heart to tell me that.

"I hated moving. Each time, I had to change schools and make new friends. Still, in every school I found a few kids I felt comfortable with and hung around at their houses—never mine, of course. Being part of a crowd helped me forget my loneliness. At the same time, I didn't have to talk to anyone in particular."

Through most of her childhood years, Sarah did not tell anybody about her family situation. "Since my relatives lived far away, I thought they couldn't help me. And at home, no one talked about Dad's problem, not even my older brother and sister. Actually, I didn't admit how much Dad's alcoholism affected me, either.

"Oddly enough, I believed my family life wasn't that awful. Dad didn't beat me or burn the house down. And though I knew my friends lived in more stable homes, I still didn't realize mine was all that strange. In my head, I had developed a weird sense of reality."

While nothing disastrous happened to Sarah or her family as a result of her father's drinking, she couldn't stop worrying about the possibilities. "I was always afraid that something terrible would occur at home. Dad would come home late and drunk, put the tea kettle on, then fall asleep with a cigarette in his mouth.

Naturally the pot burned. Luckily the house didn't. Or he drove drunk and crashed the car. I was wise enough not to ride in the car with him then, but I constantly worried he might injure himself."

Nor did she feel she could count on her parents' love and support. "By the time I was ten, Dad was disappearing for days on end. My sister told me that once, when we were at the seashore, I cried when Dad left for work after the weekend. I thought I'd never see him again.

"And I was frightened that Mom would abandon us, too. Sometimes when she had a fight with Dad she would go to a friend's house for the night, leaving us kids by ourselves."

Despite the difficulties her father's alcoholism caused, Sarah considers that she was spared, compared to others in the family. "When Dad got angry, he hit my brother and Mom but not my sister and me. Maybe I escaped because I was the youngest and a girl, or because I had the sense to get out of the way when Dad was mad. I'd slip up to my room and shut the door, then fantasize about places I could go where I'd be safe. Although I heard the yelling, I felt nothing. By age ten, my feelings were numb."

Looking back, Sarah realizes how overwhelmed her mother must have been. "When Dad drank it couldn't have been easy for her, working, raising the kids, and being anxious about him. And when my parents divorced, she was the one who kept the family together.

But at the time, I didn't see things that way. I was too angry with Mom for not giving me the support I needed. Also, I blamed her for not stopping Dad's drinking. I couldn't understand how she could let him ruin his life and ours, too. Today, I realize Mom couldn't have changed Dad's behavior, but I wish she hadn't denied his alcoholism for so long."

Finally, when she was in seventh grade, Sarah realized she needed to tell someone about her life. "I was living with too many lies and excuses, and I needed to talk. So I confided in my best friend, but unfortunately she told others. It mortified me that anyone else should know about my family. Not even my teachers had any idea of what was going on in my home, since I was too ashamed to tell them. Once I lost confidence in my friend, my distrust of people was cemented."

Today, Sarah wishes she had taken a chance and talked to an adult about her home life. "I needed someone to tell me Dad's drinking wasn't my fault and there was nothing I could do to stop it, that only Dad could control his life."

Even now Sarah says she has to work at accepting help and trusting other people. "I've gotten into the bad habit of seeing myself as being able to do everything alone. That makes it hard for anyone who works or lives with me. People don't know when to offer me a hand, and I'm not sure when to accept it. Happily, I'm starting to change that attitude. Little by little, I'm learning to trust."

While in college, Sarah started going to a therapist for help with the problems caused by her father's alcoholism. Today she belongs to Al-Anon, and "talking to the group makes me feel better," she says.

A few years ago Sarah saw her father again after a long period of separation. His appearance shocked her. "The handsome father I once knew had no teeth, was thin, and limped from a sore knee. It hurt seeing him that way, but I've come to understand that I can't lead his life. For too long I worried about Mom and Dad. Now it's time to treat myself well.

"I keep saying to myself, 'The craziness you lived with is in the past, let go of it.' Although I know the memories will always be there, I've stopped dwelling on them.

"Some people say that the best part of life is when you're a kid. Not for the child of an alcoholic who didn't get help. For me the best part of life has just started and it's improving each day."

"I never want to drink when I get older"

DAISY, age 10

"Before I was born, my mother was already drinking. I never knew much about my father because my parents divorced when I was two, and I hardly saw him after that.

"I wish Mom never drank," Daisy says wistfully. "It makes me angry thinking about it. After Dad left, there was nothing I could do once he was gone. At least, we had Mom. But she didn't take care of me the way I thought she was supposed to. I wanted a mom who took me to the park or laughed and joked with me the way other mothers did."

Daisy often felt frightened when her mother drank, especially at night, when she'd get up and hear her mother crying. "I thought she'd die and I'd never see her again," Daisy recalls. "Who would take care of me, then?"

Other nights Daisy would awaken and not find her

mother at home. "I was real young then, and thought a wizard had taken her away. I couldn't understand why she would leave me and my brother alone in the house."

Throughout this period, Daisy's mother still cooked meals for her two children. "Even though we had little money because she didn't work, Mom always fed me. But she couldn't buy me nice clothes. Nothing I wore matched. I'd go to school with brown pants and a navy shirt, then see all the other kids in pretty outfits. In kindergarten, I remember feeling so unhappy about how I looked. And when kids brought in their new toys I felt worse."

More difficult was when Daisy's mother picked her up from school at the end of the day. "Everyone stared at Mom because she looked sick. I was so embarrassed. Then she'd take me in the car, and I'd know she'd been drinking.

"I'd ask her over and over, 'When are you going to stop?' but she never seemed to hear me. It was as if Mom was somewhere else," Daisy describes. "Even my brother, Christian, who's ten years older than me, couldn't do anything. If he hid her liquor or poured it out, he knew she'd get angry and spank him, so he never tried. When Mom got mad, she hit us a lot. She doesn't do that anymore, I'm happy to say."

Daisy's not certain what made her mother finally stop drinking. But four years ago, her mother decided to go to the hospital and get detoxified.

Now she attends meetings at AA while Daisy goes to a treatment center for children of alcoholics. "I like talking to the counselor and the group leader there about my mom's drinking. They really help me. At home, I tell Mom when I feel sad, like if something bothers me at school, and she listens to me. But I only talk about Mom's alcohol problem at the treatment center. It's easier to talk about it there. Everybody understands what I'm saying. Anyway, Mom told me not to tell anyone else about her drinking. 'It's our secret,' she says. So I don't say anything to my friends. Besides, it never comes up."

Daisy doesn't think her best friend, Dawn, knows about her mother's problem. Although they spend lots of time at each other's houses, they usually don't discuss their families. "Mostly we dress up in old clothes or pretend we're cooks."

Looking back, Daisy says she always invited friends to the house, despite her mother's drinking. "It made no difference to Mom. When she drank, she'd act kind of sleepy, as if she wasn't there. She'd sit by herself and drink and smoke, without bothering anyone."

Since Daisy's mother has been sober, Daisy says, both her mother's life and her own have improved considerably. "Mom's real fun, and I like being with her. We go to the movies together or shopping for clothes. Shopping is the best. Now that she works—she cooks for a family—there's extra money, and sometimes I get treats. If Mom promises to buy me a toy, I usually can count on getting it. That doesn't mean she keeps her promises all the time, but it's different than when she drank. Today she said I could get new sneakers, but when it got too late, she said we'd go tomorrow. I was disappointed and angry, and she knew how I felt. 'Don't worry. We'll get them,' Mom said, and I know we will. I never would have believed her before.

"I look at Mom today and see her cheery most of the time. I like her that way and try to do things to make her happy. Last night I cleaned her room. She kept thanking me and hugging and kissing me. She hugs and kisses me a lot," Daisy says with a smile.

"I don't want to cause Mom any trouble, so I try hard to behave. If I have no one to play with when I come home from school, I keep busy in my room. I don't bother Mom. Lots of times, Mom tells me I'm a good kid, but I'm not so sure about that. I don't do very well in school because I have a reading problem. And I'm shy. It takes me a long time to make friends."

Although Daisy says she enjoys playing by herself, she would like to be part of a large family. "When Christian's at school, it's just Mom and me. But he comes home for vacation, and then we have more fun. We'll do something special, like go to a restaurant. Still I wish I had a bigger family with grandparents and cousins who came over. Kids who have lots of relatives are lucky, especially if they don't drink. I never want to drink when I get older—maybe just one drink at a party. That's it.

"And I'd like my job to have something to do with art, like ceramics. Or I'd like to work in a flower shop where it's pretty and smells good. I think Mom picked my name, Daisy, because I remind her of a flower."

And, Daisy adds, if she has children, she'd like to have a boy and a girl. "I can just picture my daughter," she giggles. "Helpful, cheerful, pretty, and smart. I'd want her to play all the time and be happy. And I'd like her to have brown hair and hazel eyes, just like me."

"I've got so much to look forward to each day"

SUSAN, age 40

"My family was the all-American kind you read about. Dad held an executive position at a large corporation. Mom was bright, beautiful, an outstanding lady in the community, and an excellent corporate wife. Our family had no history of alcoholism, nor was drinking part of my grandparents' lives," Susan recounts.

Yet by the time she was seven, Susan felt uncomfortable being around her mother in the evening. "She and Dad ended each day with a few drinks. They said it relaxed them, and I thought this was normal behavior. But, while Dad held his liquor well and didn't act strange, alcohol made Mom irritable and often angry. She particularly embarrassed me when my friends came over, so I made sure they didn't visit at that time."

When Susan describes her mother, it's as if she's talking about two different people: one who was capable and charming when sober; the other who was insulting when drunk. "At ten in the morning and through most of the day, Mom amazed me. She could run a convention, preside at meetings of her college alumni group, and hold a dinner party, cooking and serving everything to perfection. After her evening cocktails, she assumed another personality, flying off the handle at the slightest remark and becoming verbally abusive to anyone in her way. Mostly she picked on me, the older of her two children and the only girl."

Susan felt closer to her father and admired his soft-mannered tone and laid-back attitude. "In my mind Dad could do nothing wrong. He drank, but didn't get tipsy. He stopped smoking when he set his mind to it. Moreover, we shared similar interests, in athletics and writing. And we both were big thinkers. I thought Dad was terrific, and he thought the same of me. Looking back, I see where I got my inner strength."

Toward her mother, Susan says she felt more respect than affection. "My mother had special qualities. Whatever she did, she did well, except develop a cozy relationship with me. I suppose I contributed to that by keeping a distance," she confesses, "but Mom's drinking put me on guard. I never knew how she would act from one minute to the next."

Susan thinks her mother started drinking to be part of a social setting. "Both my parents belonged to a golf club. At the end of the day, they'd have cocktails with their friends and later more drinks with dinner. When

I was fourteen, my father died of a heart attack. A year later Mom remarried another member of the club. She and Richard, her new husband, spent most of their time there. Drinking became a regular part of their lives."

Thinking about her mother's alcoholism today, Susan says she believes it wasn't as severe as it might have been. "Mom didn't break furniture or windows. She didn't hit my brother, Tom, or me, and she never fell down. But liquor radically changed her moods, making her hurtful and abusive. Worse, it created a barrier that prevented us from getting close to each other."

When her mother drank, Susan recalls facing a barrage of criticism. "You look too skinny," her mother would say. Or, "Why is your hair so curly?"

"No matter what I said or did, she found fault. If I told her to leave me alone, she'd say I was too sensitive. To protect myself, I knew I had to keep her out of my life."

From her earliest years in school, Susan earned high grades and had many friends. "As I got older, I stayed away from the house as much as possible, filling my time with sports and after-school activities. "Thank goodness for athletics. It was an outlet for my anger. As soon as I learned to hit a tennis ball, I whacked out my feelings against the school-yard wall. Usually I felt better afterward. Today, I realize it would have been wiser to talk to a teacher or another adult, but that didn't enter my mind at the time. At least I had some way to get rid of the rage."

Despite the drinking, Susan says she could rely on her mother during the day to fix meals and act responsibly when they went shopping together or met neighbors in the street. "Mom was what you would call a closet alcoholic. Until ten years ago, when she could no longer hide it, few people knew the truth about her drinking. But I learned early on that I couldn't depend on her to have an arm ready for me when I needed comforting. She could not provide emotional support. I knew I had to take care of myself. In many ways that's helped me become independent. However, I always wished I had a regular mother who lavished me with attention and with whom I could laugh and cry."

When she was in high school, Susan became close friends with Jeanne, a popular girl in her class who also played tennis. "I loved spending time at Jeanne's house. Her parents always made me feel comfortable, and we had lots to talk about. Their enthusiasm for kids was obvious." Susan envied Jeanne for having such involved parents.

Although she felt her mother constantly criticized her, other people would tell Susan, "Your mother thinks the world of you." Now Susan says, "Apparently Mom had no difficulty bragging about my successes to others. Too bad she didn't praise me.

"And there was plenty about me to make her proud. I was a super-responsible, good kid—the favorite baby-sitter on the street. In school, the kids elected me president of the class and captain of the softball team. And at home, too, I took charge, especially after my father died. If anything went wrong in the house, I got it fixed. If my brother, Tom, needed help, I was there to solve his problem. Even now I'm amazed by my own competency. But nothing I did could win Mom's approval."

As an adult, Susan understands more about alcoholism as a disease and says she's learning to be accepting of her mother, although she still drinks. "For the past five years we've actually shared some fun together. Once Mom's husband died and she lost her drinking companion, she cut back some, but not totally. The last time my husband and I took her out for dinner, she practically fell drunk into the soup.

"I never pushed Mom to join AA, but now that she's developed a liver condition from alcoholism I talk squarely to her about her drinking. When she falls down drunk and bruises herself, I say, 'It wouldn't happen if you didn't drink so much.' I doubt she hears me, but that's her problem."

As a child, Susan says she hated her parents' drinking, but she never told them how she felt. "It's hard for a kid to do that. Deep down, I wanted to remain loyal and be loved. Still I wish I had said something," Susan admits.

"Years ago, I should have discussed my problems with Jeanne's mother or another adult. I didn't even talk to my brother about it. Had I opened up to somebody sooner, I probably would have had an easier time, but that's past and over with. At least I talk to people now."

Looking back, Susan says she was lucky to have had an unusual father for fourteen years of her life. "Dad gave me a foundation of strength and courage to build upon. But it would be unfair not to say that Mom, too, contributed to the positive parts of my personality."

Although it saddens her to see how unhappy her mother is, Susan knows that no one can change another person. "It's a shame Mom let drinking tarnish her life. She had so many attributes, but she messed up. Still, she can count on me if she's in trouble. I care about her. But I'm also taking care of myself.

"As a basically happy person, I've got so much to look forward to each day. Most of all I have strength and hope, and I'm a survivor."

BIBLIOGRAPHY

The following sources are particularly helpful for families living with an alcoholic.

For children:
Black, Claudia. *My Dad Loves Me, My Dad Has a Disease: A Workbook for Children of Alcoholics.* Denver, Co.: MAC Printing and Publications, 1982.
From viewpoint of children ages five to fourteen who have alcoholic parents. Discusses parents' personality changes, blackouts, relapses, and recovery. Child enters own feelings in actual book.

Ryerson, Eric. *When Your Parent Drinks Too Much: A Book for Teenagers.* New York: Facts on File Publication, 1985.
Coping strategies for children of alcoholics, emphasizing that the child did not cause the problem and can't control it. Stresses the importance of the child's improving his own life.

Seixas, Judith S. *Living with a Parent Who Drinks Too Much.* New York: Greenwillow, 1979.
Anecdotes from children living in an alcoholic environment and author's ideas about how to cope.

For adults:
Ackerman, Robert. *Children of Alcoholics.* Florida: Learning Publications, Inc., 1983.
Discusses the impact of a parent's alcoholism on the child. Provides insight into various behavior patterns of children of alcoholics.

Black, Claudia. *It Will Never Happen to Me.* Denver, Co.: MAC Printing and Publications, 1982.
Children of alcoholics share their experience of living in a home where a parent drinks. Includes information on where to seek help.

Moore, Jean, ed. *Roads to Recovery.* New York: Macmillan, 1986.
Gives brief descriptions of available nationwide treatment facilities.

Seixas, Judith S., and Geraldine Youcha. *Children of Alcoholism: A Survivor's Manual.* New York: Harper & Row, 1985.
Discusses how child's personality is affected by living with an alcoholic parent. Gives advice for the family on how to cope when parent is actively drinking and what to expect when parent goes into recovery.

Stark, Elizabeth. "Forgotten Victims," *Psychology Today*, January 1987.
Discusses positive and negative coping strategies of children of alcoholics, alerting these children to the risk of becoming addicted themselves.

Wegscheider-Cruse, Sharon. *Choice-Making*. Florida: Health Communications, Inc., 1985.
Describes impact of parents' drinking on children and how it affects children's lives as adults. Offers choices possible to make for a better life.

Woititz, Janet Geringer. *Adult Children of Alcoholics*. Florida: Health Communications, Inc., 1983.
Explains personality and self-image of adults who are children of alcoholics. Offers concrete ways to change negative patterns of behavior.

SOURCES OF HELP

Adult Children of Alcoholics (ACOA)
Suite 200
2522 West Sepulveda Blvd.
Torrance, CA 90505
Information on local meetings.

Al-Anon Family Group Headquarters, Inc.
P.O. Box 862
Midtown Station
New York, NY 10018–0862
24-hour answering service:
800–344–2666 (including Alaska, Hawaii, Puerto Rico, and Virgin Islands)
212–254–7230 or 7231 (New York and Canada)

Child Help's
National Child Abuse Hotline USA
800–4–A–CHILD   (800–422–4453)

The National Association for Children of Alcoholics
Suite 201
31706 Coast Highway
South Laguna, CA 92677
714–499–3889
Information and referrals for therapy and treatment programs for children of alcoholics; books and organizations;
local chapters; and support groups.

National Clearinghouse for Alcohol and Drug Information
P.O. Box 2345
Rockville, MD 20852
301–468–2600
Lists of treatment programs and information on alcohol and
drug problems.

National Council on Alcoholism
12 West 21st Street
New York, NY 10010
800–NCA–CALL

National Institute on Drug Abuse Helpline
800–843–4971
Information provided for alcohol and drug problems.

INDEX